Table of Contents

Introduction

Welcome to the wonderful world of rice! There are just so many different varieties of rice to choose from that all create delicious dishes that pack a large chunk of nutritional value. Even among the most popular varieties there is still so much to consider. Take for example white rice, which is not super nutritional but creates delicious side dishes. Or brown rice, which is far healthier as it contains magnesium and B vitamins but takes a little more care to cook properly. Then there is black rice which is the healthiest of the three, with a high value of protein and antioxidants but, the truth is not many people who what to do with it.

Ham and Pepperoni Rice Balls

You can usually find ham and pepperoni in pizza, but in this recipe, it's served as rice balls! Sweet and flavorful. Kids and adults will surely love!

Serves: 4-6

Time: 25 minutes

Ingredients:

- 2 cups of cooked white rice
- ¼ cup shredded mozzarella
- ½ cup grated parmesan
- ½ cup of diced ham or you can use pepperoni minis
- 1 cup Italian-style breadcrumbs
- 3 eggs
- Oil, for frying

Directions:

1. Preheat oil in a medium sized pot. Use enough oil to fry the rice balls, about 4 inches.
2. In a medium sized bowl, combine the parmesan, rice, mozzarella and one egg. Cool the rice first and use your hands to mold.
3. Add pepperoni or diced ham, and using your hands, combine it into the mixture

4. Form each rice ball by putting 2 tablespoons of the mixture into your hands. Press and squeeze the mixture firmly in your hands, creating a ball or circle.
5. In one small sized bowl, whisk two eggs. Place and scatter breadcrumbs in a separate dish.
6. Dip each rice ball in the egg mixture and follow it up in the breadcrumbs.
7. When the oil is hot, put 3 of the breaded rice balls to the hot pot and fry them for about 5 minutes.
8. Remove the fried rice balls from the hot oil. Transfer them to a plate with paper towel.
9. Repeat steps until you finish all the rice mixture.
10. Serve it with marinara sauce

Chinese Turkey Rice Balls

This is a great recipe that is not authentic Chinese but has some bold Chinese flavors.

Serves: 2 dozen rice balls

Time: 50 minutes

Ingredients:

- 1 lb ground turkey
- 1 small onion minced
- 2 cloves garlic minced
- 1/4 cup fresh spinach, minced
- 1 small knob of fresh ginger, minced
- 2 tbsp soy sauce
- 1 tbsp dry sherry
- 1 tsp honey
- 1 egg, lightly beaten
- 1 cup short grain rice, soaked in water for 20 minutes then drained

Directions:

1. In a large bowl, combine all the ingredients, but not the rice.
2. Wet your hands and make the meat mixture into ball shapes.
3. One at a time, roll the balls in the rice.
4. Steam balls for about 30 minutes over high heat.
5. Serve with a side of Chinese mustard.

Kim Bap (Korean Rice Rolls)

If you love sushi, try this Korean recipe. It's very healthy and delicious at the same time. Serve this with your favorite dipping sauce, and you're good to go.

Serves: 4

Time: 25 minutes

Ingredients:

- 4 cups hot cooked rice
- 1/2 teaspoon soy sauce
- 1 teaspoon rice vinegar
- 1/2 teaspoon dark sesame oil
- Carrot, 1, small, julienned
- 4 sheets kim fresh seaweed
- Eggs, 2, beaten
- 1/2 teaspoon sesame oil
- Spinach, 10 oz., frozen, thawed, drained
- 1/2 teaspoon soy sauce
- 1 tablespoon sesame seeds, toasted
- 4 slices pickled yellow radishes

Directions:

1. Let rice cool a bit.
2. Meanwhile, mix the rice with the soy sauce, vinegar and sesame oil.
3. Fry the eggs as if it were a pancake.
4. Cut the eggs into strips.
5. Mix spinach with soy sauce and sesame oil.
6. To assemble, put rice on a bamboo roller.
7. Spread the rice over 2/3 of the sheet, lay spinach, carrots and egg on top.
8. Sprinkle with sesame seeds and roll repeatedly.
9. Cut into 1/2 inch rounds.

Southwest Rice Salad

This healthy salad looks and tastes great. Also, it's very healthy so it's perfect to eat without any guilt! It tastes a little spicy, but it is very appetizing.

Serves: 6

Time: 20 minutes

Ingredients:

- 2 cups cooked rice
- 1 (12 ounce) can white corn, drained
- 1 (16 ounce) can black beans, rinsed and drained
- 1 bunch green onion, chopped
- 1/4 cup fresh squeezed lime juice (3-4 limes)
- 1/3 cup canola oil
- 2 tablespoons apple cider vinegar

- 2 -3 pickled jalapeno peppers, seeded and chopped
- 1 tablespoon packed brown sugar
- 2 teaspoons chili powder
- 2 teaspoons ground cumin

Directions:

1. In a large bowl, combine the onions, corn, beans and rice.
2. Toss to mix.
3. In a food processor, blend the remaining ingredients, until the peppers are finely minced.
4. Pour the dressing over the rice mixture and mix well.
5. Enjoy.

Nacho Supreme Rice

Nachos are very tasty, and a lot of people love it. But combined with rice? Be surprised with this entrée. The cheesy and spicy taste of nachos really goes well with the rice. Try it!

Serves: 4

Time: 10 minutes

Ingredients:

- 1 lb. ground beef
- 1 cup shredded cheddar cheese (about 4 oz.)
- 2 cups Spanish rice (cooked)
- 2 cups shredded romaine lettuce leaves
- 1 cup chopped tomato

Directions:

1. Prepare Spanish rice according to package directions.
2. Cook the ground beef in 12-inch non-stick pan over medium-high heat until it becomes brown; drain, if desired. Stir in Spanish rice.

3. Transfer rice to a serving platter, then top with tomato, lettuce and cheese and tomato.
4. Serve, and enjoy with your preferred nacho topping.

Veggie Fried Rice

This is a fried rice recipe perfect for vegetarians, and a total Chinese comfort food...in minutes!!! It's just the right amount of sweetness and saltiness from the variety of vegetables.

Serves: 2

Time: 15 minutes

Ingredients:

- 1 cup Brown rice
- ½ green pepper
- ½ small onion
- ¼ cup carrots
- 1 cup cabbage
- ½ cup broccoli
- ½ tablespoon rice wine vinegar
- 1 teaspoon garlic powder
- ½ tablespoon soy sauce
- 2 teaspoons sesame oil

Directions:

1. Prepare the rice according to the package. Set aside.
2. Dice all veggies. Heat sesame oil over medium heat and add in carrots, onions and green pepper- let it cook for 3 minutes.
3. Add in cabbage and broccoli, continuing to cook until broccoli is tender. Stir in vinegar, soy sauce and garlic powder- cook for one more minute.
4. Toss in your rice then stir occasionally while cooking for 4 minutes. Taste and season to taste with soy sauce and pepper.

Lemon Shrimp with Rice

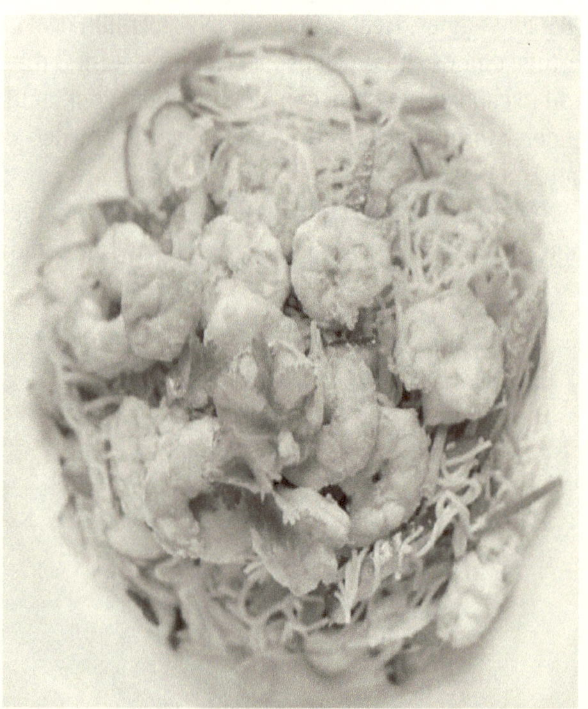

This fuss-free and delicious recipe requires only 25 minutes of preparation and requires only one dish, making cleanup a piece of cake. The tangy lemon combined with shrimp and rice is very tasty.

Serves: 4

Time: 40 minutes

Ingredients:

- 1 cup long-grain white rice
- 1 tablespoon olive oil
- 1 cup dry white wine
- 3 garlic cloves, sliced
- Coarse salt and ground pepper
- 1/4 teaspoon red-pepper flakes
- 1-pound medium shrimp, peeled and deveined
- 2 tablespoons chopped fresh parsley
- 1 lemon, cut into 8 wedges and seeded

Directions:

1. In a shallow microwave-safe dish with a lid, combine wine, rice, oil, garlic, 2 cups water and red-pepper flakes; season with salt and pepper.
2. Cover, and microwave for about 20 minutes, stirring twice during cooking.
3. Stir in lemon wedges and shrimp; cover, and microwave for 3 minutes more.
4. Let it stand, covered, for about 2 minutes. Stir in parsley; serve immediately.

Rice Stuffed Peppers

These brightly colored bell peppers, be it red or green, are a rich source of nutrients! It also looks great so it's a plus if you're designing a buffet table for the party.

Serves: 4

Time: 40 minutes

Ingredients:

- 1 package Knorr Rice Sides - Cheddar Broccoli
- 1 tbsp. butter
- 2 cups water
- 1/2 lb. ground beef
- 2 large red bell peppers

Directions:

1. Preheat the oven to 350° F.

2. Prepare Knorr Rice Sides- Cheddar Broccoli with water and follow package direction.
3. Meanwhile, cook ground beef in 10-inch pan over medium heat then drain. Add to hot rice then stir.
4. Half the peppers lengthwise and deseed them. Use your rice mixture to fill your peppers.
5. Arrange the stuffed peppers in a baking dish. Bake covered for 20 minutes. Remove cover and continue baking 10 minutes more.
6. Top with shredded cheddar cheese then serve.

Cajun Shrimp and Rice

This Cajun Shrimp and Rice is such a winner. With the tomatoes and thyme, this dish tastes so fresh and absolutely wonderful. Easy to prepare, a little spicy but that is what Cajun food is all about. Enjoy!

Serves: 4

Time: 20 minutes

Ingredients:

- 3 1/2 oz long-grain rice
- 2 lbs. large shrimp, peeled
- 2 tbsp olive oil
- 1 tbsp seasoning salt (Cajun, free)
- 1 cup bell pepper
- 1 tbsp minced garlic
- 1/4 cup green onions, chopped
- 1/2 cup Italian style stewed tomatoes
- 1/4 tsp dried thyme
- 1/2 tsp salt
- 1/8 tsp black pepper

Directions:

1. Cook rice according to package directions.
2. While the rice cooks, take a large non-stick pan and put it over

medium-high heat and add 1 tbsp of oil.

3. Sprinkle shrimp with Cajun seasoning; and toss to coat. Add shrimp to the pan; sauté for 4 minutes. Remove from pan; keep warm.
4. Heat 1 tablespoon oil in pan over medium-high heat. Add the garlic; sauté for 30 seconds. Add the green onions, thyme and pepper stir-fry; sauté for 3 minutes. Stir in shrimp, cooked rice, salt and pepper, tomatoes and cook for 1 minute.

Lemon Shrimp with Rice

This fuss-free and delicious recipe requires only 25 minutes of preparation and requires only one dish, making cleanup a piece of cake. The tangy lemon combined with shrimp and rice is very tasty.

Serves: 4

Time: 40 minutes

Ingredients:

- 1 cup long-grain white rice
- 1 tablespoon olive oil
- 1 cup dry white wine
- 3 garlic cloves, sliced
- Coarse salt and ground pepper
- 1/4 teaspoon red-pepper flakes
- 1-pound medium shrimp, peeled and deveined
- 2 tablespoons chopped fresh parsley
- 1 lemon, cut into 8 wedges and seeded

Directions:

1. In a shallow microwave-safe dish with a lid, combine wine, rice, oil, garlic, 2 cups water and red-pepper flakes; season with salt and pepper.
2. Cover, and microwave for about 20 minutes, stirring twice during cooking.
3. Stir in lemon wedges and shrimp; cover, and microwave for 3 minutes more.
4. Let it stand, covered, for about 2 minutes. Stir in parsley; serve immediately.

Chorizo and Shrimp Rice

This fried rice recipe is great for breakfast. The sweetness of the chorizo and the tenderness of the shrimp complement the rice very well, it's very savory!

Serves: 6

Time: 1 hour

Ingredients:

- 2 1/4 cups long grain brown rice
- 10 oz. small shrimp, shelled
- 3 oz. Spanish cured chorizo
- 2 cloves garlic, peeled, thinly sliced
- 1/2 cup chopped yellow onion
- 1 tablespoon canola or vegetable oil
- pinch of saffron
- 3 1/2 cups low-sodium vegetable stock or kelp stock
- 1 cup clam juice
- 1 cup fresh green peas
- 1/4 cup ginger, peeled and thinly sliced

- 1 teaspoon sea salt

Directions:

1. Rinse the rice and soak. Drain the rice and let it stay for 20 minutes to dry.
2. Place the Italian pork sausage in a pot of boiling water for 3 minutes, then drain and set aside.
3. Cut the shrimp into halves crosswise. Heat the canola oil in a pan over medium-low heat.
4. When the oil is hot throw in your onion then allow to cook for about 2 minutes. Increase heat to medium, add the saffron and garlic and cook for 20 seconds.
5. Combine the shrimp and cook just until the shrimp becomes opaque.
6. Place the clam juice, drained rice and stock in a medium sized pot. Level the rice and scatter the shrimp mixture and onion on top of the rice, then add the whole chorizo, salt and green peas. Do not stir the rice.
7. Cover the pot with a lid and cook the rice as instructed.
8. After the rice is cooked, transfer the whole chorizo to a cutting board. Cut the chorizo into half inch dice.
9. Scatter the chorizo pieces on top of the rice. Do not stir the rice at this time. Immediately cover the pot and let the rice stand for 10 minutes.
10. Remove the lid and fold the ingredients and rice together with a spatula.
11. Serve and enjoy!

Skinny Chicken Fried Rice

This recipe will save you money and give you half the calories of an expensive takeout dish. Within a few minutes, you will have a tasty, healthy, family-friendly dinner that is especially great for people with high blood pressure.

Serves: 6

Time: 20 minutes

Ingredients:

- 4 cups rice
- ½ pound boneless, skinless chicken breasts
- 1 cup peas and carrots; frozen
- 1 small, white onion
- 2 cloves garlic
- ¼ cup lite soy sauce
- 2 eggs
- 3 tbsp. sesame oil

Directions:

1. Prepare rice following package instructions to get 4 cups cooked rice.

2. Cook and chop chicken breasts into bite-size pieces.
3. Chop the onion and mince garlic cloves.
4. Set sesame oil to get hot in a large pan on medium heat.
5. Add garlic, onion, peas & carrots and fry until the veggies are tender.
6. Crack eggs into pan and scramble, mixing in with the vegetables.
7. Add chicken, rice and soy sauce to pan.
8. Mix very well.

Mixed Grain Mushroom Casserole

It's full of healthy ingredients, delectable, and is an excellent way to introduce wary folks to wild mushrooms without overwhelming them.

Serves: 8

Time: 1 hour and 15 minutes

Ingredients:

- 1/2 cup wild rice
- 1/2 cup brown rice
- 1/2 cup pearl barley
- 1/4 cup oil (or less)
- 4 garlic cloves, chopped
- 1 large onion, thinly sliced
- 4 tablespoons butter
- 3 1/2 cups broth
- 1/2 lb. mushroom, thickly sliced
- 1 teaspoon crushed dried thyme
- salt & pepper, to taste
- 1/2 teaspoon crushed dried oregano

Directions:

1. Combine grains in a mixing bowl and set aside.

2. Pour the oil into a casserole which is safe for both oven cooking and stovetop, and place on medium heat.
3. When already hot, sauté the garlic and onion until translucent and tender, for about 5 to 6 minutes.
4. Add the mixed grains and sauté for 1 minute, stir constantly.
5. Meanwhile melt the butter in a separate pan on medium high heat.
6. When already hot, add mushrooms and sauté quickly, stir frequently, until the mushrooms are hot, for about 1 minute.
7. Immediately remove from heat.
8. Add the herbs, mushrooms and broth to the casserole with the grains and onions, and bring to a boil.
9. Season with salt and pepper to taste, cover tightly, and bake at 350 degrees for 1 hour.

Meatless Hopping John

This dish is a nutritional gold mine. A colorful, tasty and filling dish. Serve this recipe with a green salad and a fruit dessert to complete your awesome meal.

Serves: 10

Time: 30 minutes

Ingredients:

- 3/4 cup long grain brown rice
- 3 medium carrots, thinly sliced
- 1 cup frozen corn
- 1/2 cup green pepper, chopped
- 1/2 cup yellow pepper, chopped (or orange)
- 1/2 cup red pepper, chopped
- 1/4 cup onion, chopped
- 1 tablespoon olive oil
- 4 garlic cloves, minced
- 1 (15 1/2 ounce) can black-eyed peas, rinsed and drained
- 2 tablespoons fresh parsley, minced
- 1 (14 1/2 ounce) can diced tomatoes, drained

- 3 teaspoons fresh thyme, chopped
- 1/4 teaspoon pepper
- 1/2 teaspoon salt
- 1/4 teaspoon crushed red pepper flakes
- hot sauce

Directions:

1. Cook the rice according to package directions.
2. Meanwhile, in a large nonstick pan, sauté the carrots, corn, onion, garlic and pepper in oil for 6 minutes or until crisp tender.
3. Stir in the rice, tomatoes and peas; bring to a boil.
4. Reduce to low heat, cover and simmer for 5 minutes, stirring occasionally.
5. Add the seasonings; cook 2 minutes longer.
6. Sprinkle hot sauce to taste.

Vegetarian Paella

Hot paella is nice to eat especially on a cold evening. It has an authentic Spanish taste. With this recipe, you can eat paella the vegetarian way, and it is also very easy to make!

Serves: 6

Time: 50 minutes

Ingredients:

- 1 pinch saffron
- 3 tablespoons authentic olive oil
- 1 medium eggplant, cut into large chunks
- 1 onion, chopped
- 1 yellow pepper, finely chopped
- 2 garlic cloves, crushed
- 1 red bell pepper, finely chopped

- 1 ½ cups Arborio rice
- 2 teaspoons paprika
- 2 1/2 cups vegetable broth
- salt and pepper
- 1 (19 ounce) can diced tomatoes
- 1 cup mushroom, sliced
- 1 (19 ounce) can chickpeas, rinsed and drained
- 1 cup green beans, cut into segments

Directions:

1. In a small bowl pour 3 tbsp of water and add in saffron and set aside.
2. Sprinkle salt on the eggplant chunks and let stand for 30 minutes. Rinse and drain.
3. Heat oil in a large pan and sauté the garlic, onion, peppers and eggplant for 5 minutes. Sprinkle and toss with paprika.
4. Add the rice, then mix the vegetable stock, saffron, tomatoes, and season with salt and pepper to taste.
5. Boil and simmer for 15 minutes, uncovered, stirring frequently.
6. Fold in the green beans, mushroom and chickpeas.
7. Cook for another 15 minutes and serve immediately.

Thai Pineapple Fried Rice

You would never guess pineapple would be this delicious with fried rice. It gives the dish a sweet flavor.

Serves: 4-6

Time: 25 minutes

Ingredients:

- 4 tablespoons vegetable oil
- 3 cloves garlic, crushed
- 1 onion, finely chopped
- 1 cup finely chopped carrot
- 1 cup fresh pineapple chunks or canned pineapple chunk, drained
- 1 cup finely chopped green beans
- 1 tablespoon ketchup (or tomato puree)

- 3 cups cold cooked rice
- 1 teaspoon salt
- 4 tablespoons chopped green onions
- 1 cucumber, thinly sliced
- 4 tablespoons chopped fresh cilantro

Directions:

1. In a pan, heat oil over medium heat and stir-fry garlic and onion until golden brown.
2. Add the green beans and carrots and stir-fry for 2 minutes.
3. Add rice, pineapple, salt and ketchup mixing well and stir-frying for 3 minutes.
4. Garnish with cilantro and green onion before serving.

5. Serve with soy sauce, if desired.

Spanakorizo Risotto

Spinach's is considered a superfood for good reason. The large amount of nutrients it contains helps promote bone, skin and eye health as well as healthy blood pressure. This healthy risotto is great to go with feta cheese or crusty bread. Enjoy!

Serves: 4

Time: 31 minutes

Ingredients:

- 1 1/2 lbs. spinach, cleaned, stemmed, torn
- 1 cup chopped spring onion
- 1/2 cup olive oil
- 1 small onion, chopped
- rice, 1 1/4 cups, short-grain
- 1 leek, chopped
- lemon juice, 1/4 cup
- 3 cups water
- 2 tablespoons minced fresh dill
- salt
- fresh ground black pepper
- 1 tablespoon tomato paste (optional)

Directions:

1. In a deep pan heat the oil and gently fry the onion and leek until soft.
2. Wash rice, drain and add to onion.
3. Cook for 5 minutes, stirring frequently.
4. Add the remaining ingredients, except spinach, and boil. Cook for 10 more minutes.
5. Add the spinach, stir it well and then cover.
6. Reduce heat and simmer on low heat for 5-6 minutes.
7. Remove from heat.
8. Leave the lid on and let it stand at least 30 mins before serving.

Spanish Chicken and Rice Bake

A throw-it-together and pop it in the oven supper. Enjoy this fresh-tasting, well-seasoned chicken casserole recipe.

Serves: 4

Time: 55 minutes

Ingredients:

- 10oz canned cream of chicken soup
- Water, 1/2 cup
- 1 cup salsa
- 1 cup whole kernel corn
- 4 boneless chicken breast halves
- 3/4 cup uncooked long-grain white rice
- 1/2 teaspoon chili powder

- black beans, 1 cup, canned, washed
- 1/2 cup shredded cheddar cheese

Directions:

1. Mix soup, water, salsa, beans, corn and rice in a shallow baking dish.
2. Top with chicken that is seasoned with pepper and salt, then sprinkle with chili powder.
3. Cover it with casserole lid or foil.
4. Bake at 375°F for 45 minutes.
5. Sprinkle with cheese.

Benihana Japanese Fried Rice

This recipe is very tasty; it's just like the usual fried rice, but Japanese style. This is perfect for breakfast.

Serves: 4

Time: 20 minutes

Ingredients:

- 4 cups cooked rice or 1 cup uncooked rice
- 2 tablespoons carrots, finely diced
- 1 cup frozen peas, thawed
- 2 eggs, beaten
- 1 1/2 tablespoons butter
- 1/2 cup onion, diced
- 2 tablespoons soy sauce
- pepper
- salt

Directions:

1. Cook rice following instructions on package (Boil 2 cups of water, add a dash of salt and rice, and cook for 20 minutes).

2. Pour rice into a large sized bowl to let it cool.
3. Allow your eggs to scramble on medium heat in a small pot.
4. Crush the scrambled eggs into small bits that are pea sized while you cook.
5. When rice has cooled to room temperature, put in the grated carrot, peas, diced onion and scrambled egg to the bowl.
6. Mix all of the ingredients together.
7. Over medium heat, melt the butter in a large frying pan.
8. When the butter has melted, mix the other ingredients and rice into the pan and add pepper, salt and soy sauce.
9. Allow the rice to cook for about 6 minutes, stirring often.

Beef Taco Rice

Taco combined with rice is heavenly. This is great for lunch or dinner. If there are leftovers, wrap them up in a flour tortilla to serve for lunch the next day.

Serves: 5

Time: 31 minutes

Ingredients:

- 1 lb. ground beef
- 1 1/2 cups water
- 1 (1 1/4 ounce) envelope taco seasoning mix
- 1 cup thick & chunky salsa
- 1 1/2 cups uncooked instant rice
- 1 cup frozen whole kernel corn
- 3/4 cup shredded taco blend cheese

- 1 medium tomato, chopped
- 1 cup shredded lettuce
- sour cream, if desired

Directions:

1. Allow the beef to cook over medium heat in a 10-inch pan for about 10 minutes, while stirring, until brown then drain.
2. Stir in water, seasoning mix, corn and salsa. Heat until it boils then stir in rice. Boil for 1 minute; remove from heat. Cover and let it stand for 8 minutes.
3. Fluff the rice mixture with fork; sprinkle with cheese. Cover and let it stand for 2 minutes.
4. Sprinkle lettuce around the edge of pan; sprinkle the tomato in circle next to the lettuce. Serve with sour cream.

Shrimp Etouffeé

There are lots of ingredients for this recipe but with so many complex flavors you get incredible flavors that really complement one another! Enjoy the thick gravy like sauce and the tenderness of the shrimp.

Serves: 6

Time: 1 hour 35 minutes

Ingredients:

- 1/2 cup butter
- 1 cup thinly sliced green onion
- 1/4 cup all-purpose flour
- 1 cup chopped yellow onion
- 1/2 cup chopped celery
- 1/2 cup chopped bell pepper (red or yellow)
- 2 garlic cloves, minced
- 1/4 teaspoon dry thyme leaves
- 1 bay leaf
- 1/2 teaspoon dry basil leaves
- 1 cup dry white wine

- 1 (8 ounce) can tomato sauce
- 1 (8 ounce) bottle clam juice
- 1 tablespoon Worcestershire sauce
- 1/2 cup water
- 1/2 teaspoon white pepper
- 1 tablespoon grated lemon peel
- 1/4-3/4 teaspoon liquid hot pepper sauce
- 1 tablespoon lemon juice
- 1/4 cup chopped fresh parsley
- 1 1/2 lbs. cooked shrimp
- 4 -6 cups hot cooked rice

Directions:

1. Melt the butter in a 5 quart pan over medium heat. Stir in the flour until bubbly. Stir in yellow onion, green onion, bell pepper, garlic, celery, bay leaf, basil and thyme.
2. Reduce the heat to low and cook uncovered, stirring often for about 20-30 minutes.
3. Add the wine, tomato sauce, clam juice, Worcestershire sauce, water, white pepper and hot pepper sauce to taste. Bring to a boil while stirring over high heat.
4. Turn down the heat and simmer uncovered, stirring occasionally, until reduced for about 45 minutes.
5. Stir in lemon juice, lemon peel, parsley and shrimp. Simmer until shrimp are heated through.
6. Serve over hot cooked rice.

Spicy Lime Chicken with Spanish-Style Rice

It has a spicy and tangy flavor combination. This is a quick and spicy delicious main dish that you can serve as lunch or dinner. Try it!

Serves: 4

Time: 1 hour 20 minutes

Ingredients:

To make Spicy Lime Chicken:

- 24oz. chicken breast halves, bone-in, skinned
- 1/2 tsp. ground cumin
- lime juice, 1/3 cup
- 1/2 tsp. chili powder
- Cooking Spray
- 1/8 tsp. cayenne pepper

To make Spanish Style Rice:

- 1 cup uncooked rice
- 1 medium onion, chopped
- 2 tablespoons vegetable oil
- 2 1/2 cups water
- 8 oz. canned tomato sauce
- 1/8 tsp. garlic powder
- 1 1/2 tsp. salt
- 3/4 tsp. chili powder
- green bell pepper, 1 small, chopped

Directions:

To make Spicy Lime Chicken:

1. Place the chicken in a plastic zip-loc bag; pour the lime juice on the chicken. Close the bag, and shake it until the lime has coated the chicken all over. Let it marinate in the fridge for an hour, turning the bag occasionally.
2. Combine chili powder, cumin and red pepper in a small sized bowl. Remove chicken from marinade. Sprinkle the chicken with cumin mixture.
3. Use your cooking spray to coat your broiler pan rack.
4. Add your chicken with the skin faced down on your rack then set to broil for about 25 minutes. Flip the chicken pieces, and continue broiling for another 15 additional minutes or until done. Serve with Spanish-Style Rice.

To make Spanish Style Rice:

5. In a large pan, heat the oil over medium heat.
6. Add rice and onion and cook for about 5-10 minutes. Stir occasionally, until the rice is golden brown and the onion is tender.
7. Stir and let the remaining ingredients boil.
8. Reduce the heat, cover for about 30 minutes, stir occasionally, until the rice is tender.

Brown Rice Jambalaya

This dish is a classic of New Orleans and it is a perfect one-pot dinner for any event.

Serves: 5

Time: 1 hour 41 minutes

Ingredients:

- 1 tablespoon olive oil
- 1 large onion, chopped
- 12 ounces Andouille sausage, sliced
- 1 large green bell pepper, seeded and chopped
- 2 medium cloves garlic, peeled
- 2 celery stalks, diced

- 5 ounces skinless and boneless chicken breast cut into 2-inch chunks
- ½ teaspoons paprika
- 1/2 teaspoon cayenne pepper
- One 28-ounce can diced tomatoes
- 1 large bay leaf
- One 8-ounce can tomato sauce
- 2 cups chicken or seafood stock
- ¾ pound shrimp, peeled and deveined
- 1 1/2 cup brown rice
- 4 scallions, thinly sliced

Directions:

1. Heat the olive oil in a large saucepan over high heat. Add the sausage and cook until browned on both sides. Remove to a plate.
2. Turn the heat down to medium and add the bell pepper, onion and celery. Sauté for about 5 minutes. Stir in the garlic and cook for another minute.
3. Push the vegetable mixture to the sides of the pan and add the chicken. Cook the chicken, stirring occasionally, for about 5 minutes.
4. Stir in the paprika, cayenne and 1 teaspoon of salt and toss to combine. Pour the tomato sauce, tomatoes and the bay leaf over the meat mixture. Simmer uncovered for 5 minutes.
5. Add the stock and bring to a boil. Stir in the rice; reduce the heat to medium-low, and cook, covered, until the rice is tender, for 45 minutes to 1 hour.
6. Add the half of the scallions and shrimp to the pot and toss to combine. Cover and cook until the shrimp are pink and cooked through, for about 5 minutes. Ladle into bowls and garnish with the remaining scallions.

Chicken Tikka Masala Rice Bowl

This recipe has a very few ingredients so it also saves you money.

Serves: 4

Time: 25 minutes

Ingredients:

- 1 tbsp olive oil
- cooked rice
- 1 1/2 cups tikka masala curry sauce from a bottle
- 2 lbs. chicken breasts (boneless, cubed)
- 3 tbsp cilantro (chopped)

Directions:

1. Add your oil in a pan over medium heat.

2. Add in your chicken then cook while stirring until it's thoroughly cooked.
3. Add the curry sauce, make sure the chicken is well-coated by it.
4. Serve over cooked rice. Garnish with cilantro.

Baja Black Beans, Corn and Rice

This is a mix of textures and flavors. Serve this hot as a side dish with grilled meat or chicken or as a main dish.

Serves: 6

Time: 15 minutes

Ingredients:

- brown rice, 6 cups, cooked
- corn, 15 oz., canned, drained
- black beans, 15 oz., canned rinsed and drained
- 4 fresh tomatoes, diced
- 1/2 cup cilantro, chopped
- 1/2 cup red onion, chopped
- 1 jalapeno pepper, seeded and diced
- olive oil, 1 tbsp.
- lime juice, 2 tbsp.
- 1/2 tsp. salt
- 2 dashes hot sauce
- 1/4 tsp. fresh ground pepper

Directions

1. Cook the rice. In a medium sized bowl, combine all the
    ingredients.
2. To serve, place a scoop of rice on a plate, top with a scoop of the
    black bean mixture.
3. Stir together before eating.

Chicken Jalfrezi with Rice

This is a Pakistani recipe that is has lots of taste, with loads of spices. It's got a traditional taste and lots of extra vegetable thrown in.

Serves: 6

Time: 1 hour 34 minutes

Ingredients:

- 2 tablespoons vegetable oil
- 1 onion, grated
- 1 1/2 pounds boneless skinless chicken thighs
- 2 cloves garlic, chopped
- 3 teaspoons ground turmeric
- 1 1/2 teaspoons salt
- 1 teaspoon chili powder
- 2 tablespoons ghee (clarified butter)
- 1 (14.5 ounce) can peeled and diced tomatoes
- 3 teaspoons ground cumin
- 2 tablespoons grated fresh ginger root
- 3 teaspoons ground coriander
- 1/2 cup chopped cilantro leaves
- 1/2 cup long grain rice
- 1 cup water

Directions:

1. Cook the rice. Boil, cover it with lid and reduce to low heat.
2. Simmer, and stir for every 5 minutes until rice is tender, for about 20 minutes. Set the rice aside.
3. Heat the oil in a large sized pan over medium-high heat. Add the garlic and onion, and cook for about 2 minutes. Add the chicken, and season with chili powder, salt and turmeric. Fry gently.
4. Pour in the tomatoes and juice; then cover and simmer over medium heat for 20 minutes.
5. After that, without the lid, simmer for 10 minutes more. Add the cumin, ghee, ground coriander, cilantro, and ginger, and simmer for another 7 minutes. Serve with rice.

Island Rice Pudding

A deliciously sweet and filling rice pudding. It will be a great dessert that everyone will surely love. You can top it with any fruit that you want.

Serves: 8

Time: 25 minutes

Ingredients:

- 2 cups water
- 1 pinch salt
- 1 cup arborio rice
- 2 cups milk
- 1 teaspoon cinnamon
- 1/4-1/2 cup sugar
- Ginger, 1 tbsp., grated

- Coconut, 1 cup, shredded, dried
- Raisins, 1/2 cup
- papaya, diced, 1 cup

Directions:

1. Bring water to a boil in a medium saucepan. Add salt and rice. Cover and cook on low heat, for about 15 minutes.
2. Stir in milk and cook uncovered, stirring often until it's been reduced by half. Stir in the cinnamon, sugar, raisins and ginger.
3. Continue to cook until the rice is soft. Add your coconut, then stir. Gently fold in the papaya.
4. Taste and adjust the level of sugar to match your preferred taste.
5. Serve warm or place to chill.

Chocolate Cherry Arroz

A yummy dessert that your kids or kids at heart will surely love! Super easy to make, and the sweetness is just right.

Serves: 3

Time: 30 minutes

Ingredients:

- 3 cups water
- 1 tablespoon vanilla
- 2 cinnamon sticks
- 1 1/2 cups long grain rice
- 1 cup milk
- 1 cup dried cherries
- 1 can sweetened condensed milk
- 3 Mexican chocolate disks

- 1 can media crema

Directions:

1. In a pot with medium heat add in water, vanilla and cinnamon sticks. Bring to a boil.
2. Add in dried cherries and rice. Mix to combine, then bring to a boil.
3. Once boiling, lower the flame to a simmer and cover with a lid.
4. Simmer the rice for 20 minutes.
5. Once rice is cooked, discard the cinnamon sticks and remove the rice from flame. Allow rice to rest for a few minutes.
6. While rice is resting, in a separate pot with medium low heat, mix together Mexican chocolate disks and media crema. Mix until fully dissolved. Set the mixture aside.
7. In a large sized bowl, add in cooked rice and milk, cherries, chocolate sauce and sweetened condensed milk.
8. Mix to combine and serve either cold or warm. Enjoy!

Rice Tojeras

These Chilean pancakes are a healthier option for those who are craving for pancakes. Great for a weekend brunch that will impress your friends!

Serves: 12

Time: 25 minutes

Ingredients:

- 3 cups cooked rice
- 2 teaspoons baking powder
- 8 tablespoons flour
- 4 tablespoons powdered sugar
- 1 teaspoon cinnamon
- 2 eggs
- 3/4 cup milk
- pinch of salt

Directions:

1. Heat oil and fry in a large nonstick pan.
2. In a bowl place the baking powder, flour, cinnamon and powdered sugar.
3. Combine your eggs and milk in another bowl then whisk well.
4. Pour your egg mixture onto the flour, then stir well.
5. Add in your rice while stirring.
6. Heat the pan and oil over medium heat. Pour your batter into the pan in ¼ cup servings then cook for 8 minutes until you see bubbles blow up, repeat, cook 4 at a time when the pan is large enough.
7. Flip and cook for 7 minutes on the other side. They should be golden brown and cooked to medium, it is good to sacrifice one and try.
8. Top with condensed milk, Nutella, palm honey or powdered sugar.
9. Serve and enjoy.

Torta de Pastores

This dish is popular during Christmas season. The sweet and salty taste of this dessert complements one another.

Serves: 12

Time: 45 minutes

Ingredients:

- rice pudding, 4 cups
- butter, 1/4 cup, melted
- sponge cake crumbs, 3 cups
- white cheese, 3/4 cup, shredded
- cinnamon, 2 tsp., ground
- 4 large eggs, beaten
- raisins, 1/2 cup, soaked in warm water for 30 minutes, drained
- nutmeg, 1/4 tsp., ground
- vanilla, 1 tsp., extract
- Moscatel or Oporto wine, 1/2 cup
- Pinch of salt

Directions:

1. Set your oven to preheat to 325°F and use butter to grease a large baking pan.
2. Toss in your remaining ingredients and mix well until well combined.
3. Pour the mixture into the pan and bake it for about 30 minutes.
4. Transfer the pan to a rack and let it stand for about 15 minutes, then transfer your cake to a serving plate. Serve warm or cold.